Merlin's Message

"REAWAKENING AND REMEMBERING"

By Marelin the Magician

Published by:

Serious Comedy Publications
Post Office Box 747
Tujunga, Ca 91043

Copyright 1998

First Printing 1998

Library of Congress Catalog Card number:
97-091214
ISBN 1-891411-00-4 (pbk.)

Cover Art/Power Within
by Ann Van Eps © 1989

This book is dedicated to Sasha.

Livication

I appreciate and acknowledge:

My teachers from nonphysical and my friends in the physical: John Philip Luebsen, my living Merlin; Rudy Crusat, for his undying love and encouragement to share this message with the many rather than the few; Ann Van Eps, my magical soul sister and awesome artist; Paula Sirois, editor extraordinaire; beautiful Sharon Lee Jones, the consummate creative organizer; Ken Shaw and Ken Abel, brilliant book makers; Michael Asgariani, for his unconditional love and support; Kevin Kamali for his knowledge of desktop publishing; and

Ray West, computer wizard. I am grate-
ful to each for their part in the
cocreation of Merlin's Message. And, I
thank you, the reader, for attracting this
message.

TABLE OF CONDIMENTS...

Forward

by Lord Luebsen

*Now is the time
of the feminine emergence.*

*Now is the time
for all of us,
male or female,
to allow and receive.*

*Grace is our natural inheritance.
Ecstacy our natural state.*

*Marelin is the heart of Merlin.
She is here now to assist you
in loving yourself more fully.
She loves you unconditionally.*

Join her,
and awaken to the joy
of creating the life you want.

Magic is the Rule
and you are the Ruler.

Introduction from the author, Marelin the magician.

The message that transformed my world is age old. It came back to me in the moment I asked my Self a simple question: Being that we each create our own reality, how can we refine our abilities as Conscious Creators? Since the Universal Law of Attraction (that which is like unto itself is drawn) is continually in effect, I drew to myself the precise information that was to set me free. I have come to know, through my experience, that life can be all that we dream it can be. We indeed are continually creating our realities, whether or not we do so consciously.

As you begin to journey through this book, let your *in*tuition be your guide. The information contained herein is a key to manifesting your heart's desires. The principles I share here are invaluable tools that have worked amazing feats in my life. And, because the Laws of Creation are absolutely unwavering, these principles will undoubtedly fit beautifully within your realm of experience as well. If, as you read these words, you have a sense that they resonate with your *in*nate knowing, that is, if it feels good, then your guidance system is saying, "YES, that's it!" Pay attention within, for *you* are the complete authority of your life. What I say is so for me, and I continually reap the harvest thereof. This is the avenue through which grand and glorious things have come to me.

When I finally got it, when I truly understood that I can and do create my reality moment by moment, I began to do so with deliberate intent. My expanded awareness of the art of conscious creation has spelled liberation for me. Every day that message becomes increasingly clear. It is my knowing that this is how the Law operates in each of our lives. May these words plant the seed of conscious creation in your experience,

so that you, too, will come to feel the infinite power that dwells within you.

RETURN TO
YOUR POWER

Your life force flows
to you. . .through you.
You came forth from nonphysical
into physical form,
resonating vibrations
through feelings
that create.
Thoughts magnetized
by your focused attention are
points of creation!

Through diversity and contrast,
you make choices

that define your experience.
By allowing and loving all
experiences and conditions,
you become one with
unconditional love.
Visualize and then recognize
your creation as your manifestation.
Living life in the Now. . .
This is your point of Power!

THE CREATOR IS YOU!

Excalibur

The most powerful magical sword
in all the land
...handed down from the
dawn of man
The two-edged sword of Truth:
one edge calls forth the
flow from your power Source...
and the other cuts it off.

*Will you call it forth
or cut if off?
This is your eternal choice
as a creator!*

Young Arthur innocently approached the sword and swiftly freed it from the stone without hesitation. He had no expectations of failure, for he had no fears about the outcome. His power was in pure play, not in the torment of twisted possibilities. No yearning there, simply wonder: "What if...?" Those who failed to free the sword came to the scene with great seriousness and anxiety. Their physical force was lacking nonphysical power.

When you feel negative emotion, the sword

remains stuck in the stone, for you have cut off the flow of your creative Life Force. The sword of truth is freed from the stone when you feel positive emotion. When you choose to feel good, you allow energy to flow through you to those things that you desire. You have attained creative control of your kingdom.

You are the monarchs of Universal Source, the creators of your own Royal destiny. The inner realm is where you create the outer world. Wield your sword with the Light of Love and awaken to a life of living happily ever after, for this is truly your Royal birthright.

ONCE UPON
COUNTLESS TIMES. . .

You were born into physical form from
the nonphysical realm of existence.
From the womb of love and wisdom you
came forth as Daughter or Son of
Source, Universal Royalty. You are the
Royal Majesty of Creation, a spiritual
manifestation. You are an extension of
Creative Life Force, a solar ray of

Source energy, an aspect of the Infinite, a spark of the Divine. This is who you are, where you came from and where you always return.

From your nonphysical perspective, you recognized physical life as a thrilling creative adventure. When you projected a thought of yourself as physical, you knew that not only do you create the *way* you look at things, you create the very things you see.

After your physical emergence, you began to see the infinite choices of this earthly realm. Some things you definitely desired, and others you did not. People around you were on their guard;

they sought to avoid or exclude a life that was hard. They were watching out for what they feared to have in their experience. Soon you began to vibrate, through your feelings, with this perspective of fear. The more you noticed the things you didn't want, the more things you didn't want were drawn into your experience.

You began to doubt yourself, as you recognized that you must be doing something wrong. Feelings of unworthiness had you thinking that you did not belong. You began to look outside of yourself for your Source of connectedness. In time, you turned to others for answers and approval. You began to get caught up in how others flowed, instead of following your own flow to where you wanted to go.

Soon you were going in the opposite direction of your highest intention, having temporarily forgotten that within you lies the key to joy. You became entangled in a mire, forgetting your true desire. You engaged in a struggle whenever you tried to get away from what you didn't want.

You create what you are looking for by opening the inner door. You find yourself moving in the direction of your desired experience, when you create the feeling first within.

MAGIC MADE MANIFEST IS FULLY FELT FIRST!

You are being called to remember your joyous origins as a lover. You are an uplifter of consciousness; allow your love to flow freely as one who assists others in finding their joy. Resonate in harmony with love that is unconditional, for this is the stuff of nonphysical dimensions, and the blending of the two is bliss. Look to the Source within that you may again be filled with wonder and delight at the endless surprises the Universe has in store.

***The polarities serve you well by
providing a point of reference with
which to choose a preference.*** All these
things you forgot to remember.

Because you were often told that you
couldn't have what you wanted, you tried
to make things happen rather than envi-
sioning them *first*. This is when your joy
bubbles started to burst. The pain of
seeming separation from yourself felt
extremely unnatural to you in the beginning. In time, it began to feel normal.
This world you had created appeared to
be telling you to limit yourself. As a
physical being, you had moved away
from your original intent, to remain connected to your nonphysical flow. You

were no longer listening to or following your heart, your joy, your bliss, your excitement. You simply forgot to go with that inner flow while creating to your heart's content. At times you felt empty, like something was missing.

Hell is your state of mind, if you are making unhappiness your haven. Hell is simply the absence of heaven, and heaven is found in your joy. In that state you are connected with your Inner Being, the Source from which you came forth, and that is fulfilling your purpose. Life's meaning is found through play. You will come into your power more fully by playing in the *real*m of your imagination.

IMAGINATION IS CREATION

Imagine that the so-called Big Bang was actually the Universe having an orgasm, upon realizing it was coming into experiencing itself. ALL THAT IS did not know itself because it was ALL THERE WAS. There was no differentiation within the Self to allow it to know that another part of Self could exist. The first recognition by All That Is of itself was the first split in what is called Creation. As All One, it blissfully wanted to experience even more ecstasy, so it split itself in two and began loving self as the perfect reflection of Self. It felt so good, it split again, and then again...and yet again, ad infinitum. Source went beyond itself to yield greater and greater levels of Beingness, to expand beyond What Is, for ever and ever. Countless babies were born as Creators throughout eternity... each and every One a seed of Source, a product of that orgasmic Big Bang. With this knowing, how can you ever feel yourself to be anything less than Royalty?

If you have been told that your imagination is not real, it is time to reawaken:

Know that your imagination creates all things you call *REAL*. When you fully sense the unlimited power of your imagination, you recognize that you are Truly living your dream. *The more consciously you experience this dream, the more your dreams become your conscious experience.*

When you love yourself, you give yourself what you want. Let me show you the way. Here is where the power of your imagination comes into play. Things don't come to you just because you want them. They come to you, through you, as you energetically experience them within.

NOTHING HAPPENS TO YOU, EVERYTHING HAPPENS THROUGH YOU.

Let's play more in the *real*m of your imagination. A simple example demonstrates the importance of your existence. Just imagine that everything around you, your entire world, is not there. You are out in space, free, alone. Now, what is it that you are left with? You are simply wandering through the emptiness of unlimited space. Now imagine that you no longer exist. Go ahead; see yourself as gone, nonexistent. Do you see that it can't be done? Notice that you can imagine everything outside of yourself to be removed from the picture, but you cannot see yourself erased. You simply cannot take YOU away. YOU ARE CONSCIOUSNESS, and all consciousness, whether nonphysical or physical, is nothing more or less than "I AM."

It is all a dream or a hologram you create around your point of view. From this place of you being All That Is, where nothing else exists, you are free to place all that you want, desire or prefer into your experience. Now, as you set out to fill your world with your creations, would you choose to put things into your world that you did not want? No, of course not. That is what makes you feel less than good...and, often, downright bad. It is painfully unfulfilling. Now is the time to play at being the Creator that you came forth to Be. Envision your life as you want it to be. ***Your power is in your images; make them fun!***

When you are contained within an experience, you are that experience. If you find yourself in a state of longing/yearning to obtain something, you have energetically separated yourself from your desire, and it can never be! If you see that you don't have something, know that you are creating it to be so. What you say is so! You have to BE it to see it, so BE it! When you are flowing with your highest good, your options are limitless.

In the continuing ebb and flow of evolution, you are reawakening to your True identity and the reason you have come to Earth. Know that you are nothing more and nothing less than "I AM," the all-inclusive Supreme energy force. Connected in Oneness, we are all for one and one for all!

The magnificence of this dream called physical reality can be fully appreciated when you become aware of the infinite power contained within a single phrase. When you state: "I Am," All That Is becomes focused through a single physical point of view. That "I" is creation, for it cannot be otherwise! You are claiming your identity. Who will you create yourself to be? Investigate the realm of the infinite in your imagination.

Know that you are brave explorers on the furthest edge of Universal Consciousness, where All That Is benefits immensely from your remembrance of your TRUE identity. Your connection to Source Energy brings you bliss and ecstasy, the purpose of your quest. Your quest is to go with what feels best.

FOR YOUR INFORMATION, FRIENDS . . .

In your current version of reality, consciousness does not come forth from physicality; physicality emerges from the sea of consciousness. You chose to come forth from your nonphysical state, because you wanted to have an adventure in the physical realm. You knew this physical playground would present a joyous opportunity for growth. You set forth your intention to experience the soul's evolution. You planned to bring forth deeper awareness and insight, to allow your dreams to take flight. And to do this best, you must sit at the helm of your ship, Creator.

There is no con*damn*ation from on high. Divine Love knows no limits, has no restrictions and never condemns. It just IS and supports you unconditionally in your expression of creativity. You are of the family of Universal Royalty. Act the part, for it is written in your heart. You are here to thrive, not just survive. Some may call you selfish, but your life must be so important to you that you live it *for you.* If you don't respect yourself, how can that be mirrored back to you? *You cannot be given, nor can you give, what you do not have.*

Earth is not a school, contrary to popular belief. View it is an abundant tool shop. Simply shop around what for excites you. Your quest for fulfillment is not a test. The Spiritual Emergence Broadcast System says: this is not a test of your faith or worthiness. You do not have lessons to learn, nor do you have anything to earn. Heaven is right here. Know that you already have all you require and desire. It is your birthright as Royal heirs. Royalty does not go without; that is not what you are about. Who you are is what thrills and excites you. It only takes a bit of introspection, to recognize you want to follow that direction.

You do not have debts of karma, and regret does not serve anyone well. That is just a self-made hell. Where is the joy of this ride, if you use guilt as your guide? You are always loved unconditionally, and you are always going in the right direction, even if it seems all wrong. Remember that you can never be wrong or be wronged. Although, if you hold on tightly to such a view, you will be proved right, by your own self-fulfilling prophecy.

In Truth, there is no separation between you and anything that you want. Simply by allowing the creative wizard within you to come forth and play, you will come to see that you have one foot on Royal land and the other in the force of the invincible invisible.

For you never fail; you only grow, and that is all you need to know. Shame and blame bring more of the same. Know that there is nothing that you or anyone else is not capable of being! Do you not sense that this thought is freeing?

There is no need for justification, apology or greed. There is no right or wrong, good or bad, heaven or hell, other than what you perceive or view as such. If you see aspects of yourself that you feel are not very pretty, and you love them anyway, heaven knows your beauty grows. Appreciate those aspects of self. Depreciation holds little worth. Love all conditions, for they have brought you to where you are, and they will carry you very far. Where you are is the only place that can take you to where you want to be. You are moving to that glorious state of consciousness that is unconditional love. For, as you love and allow that which you would rather not see, you will find yourself seeing less and less of it.

THE ROYAL RULE OF REFLECTION

While here on Earth, there is only one
rule that will show you all there is to
know. For all of life is a mirror, and what
I mean is easily seen in the ROYAL
RULE OF REFLECTION. Your outer
physical reality is only a reflection of
who you are experiencing yourself to
be...no more, no less. What you are being is what you are seeing. All reality is

reflective of your relationship to every-thing. How you see it is how you get it. You are always empowering any reality you choose to reflect upon, so why not wield your power Royally?

If you are not experiencing something in your outer world, you are not experienc-ing it in your inner world. The world within is where all magic must begin. So, if your vision has yet to appear, the reason is always clear. If you find that a desire is not manifesting anywhere, understand that you are not creating yourself to be there. Within you there is no trace of lack or need. You can have anything you dream of, for your infinite supply has always been within. If you are humming in harmony with the tune of having something, and it does not flow, relax. Know that in time it will be so, or it is simply not where you are meant to go. It is not the clearest reflection of your highest intention.

Consider that three hundred billion galaxies were discovered recently. This same energy that has created infinite galaxies flows through you. You are a being of tremendous power, and you are never given a desire without also being given the ability to fulfill that desire! Your awareness of that brings it to you with *light*-ening speed.

With enough of you projecting thoughts for planetary change, you could quite literally see projected outcomes rearrange. What begins as a thought, desire, dream or fantasy is actually moving matter beyond what has been. You are extremely important in the evolution of All That Is. You are worthy, simply because you are. As you evolve within, you expand All That Is beyond what has been. Every aware move, every conscious thought, brings you into greater harmony with the physical reality you want.

You are the one who holds the vision, be it clouded or clear. Use your conscious mind to bring forth what you hold dear. **Whatever you are feeling is what you**

will be getting, and what you are getting is reflective of how you have been feeling. *If you choose to see the positive in things, you will have more positive things to see.* As anything goes out from you, it reflects back to you. Your world is a mirror. If you don't like the reflection, simply reflect upon something else.

MIRROR, MIRROR
ON THE WALL,
I AM THE ONE WHO
CREATES IT ALL.

PHILOSOPHIZING PHYSICS

As you enter the next millennium, you are seeing the bridging of Heaven and Earth once again. You are discovering more and more that science and religion, physics and philosophy are intimately interlinked.

As far as the telescope can see and as far into microscopic worlds as you can go, the continuity is clear. There is no beginning and no end, *for when you look for something new, you create it to be found.*

Physicists have now repeatedly documented that subatomic particles behave differently when observed by different people. Quarks and neutrinos often move in concordance with the thought of the observing scientist. Albert Einstein said that all matter stems from thought. Science has verified that all matter can be measured as varying frequencies of electromagnetic vibration. We know that the speed of the vibration increases as it moves from dense matter up through sound, then through the spectrum of light from infrared through ultraviolet and then to the higher finer frequencies, which we call *thought*.

Emotions and feelings are associated with all thoughts. Thoughts form into mass, and that mass becomes matter. As you send forth your strong desires, your emotions radiate electromagnetic energy that ripples endlessly throughout the entire Universe. You have set nonphysical energy into motion that forms mass, and that mass becomes physical matter. You have called forth that which is the perfect reflection of what you are radiating, by your very emanating eminence! You have launched a creation, Creator!

Things that you desire resonate at a high speed of vibration when they harmonize with your highest intention. If, through thought or deed, you go in the opposite direction of your desire, you literally slow down that vibration, and you feel negative emotion. Negative creating is what you do when you focus on LACK in front of you. *You do this when you want something you don't see, or if you have something that you don't want to see.* What persists is what you resist, so change the direction of the flow, and take it where you want to go. *In the game of life...*

...YOU CANNOT SCORE A TOUCHDOWN IF YOU ARE RUNNING IN THE OPPOSITE DIRECTION OF THE GOAL LINE.

When energy moves in a direction counter to any desire, it causes resistance, and that resistance causes dis-ease. When you turn the energy in the direction that causes easing, dis-ease falls away. The moment that you begin to question your health or abundance, you plant a seed of doubt that is sure to sprout.

Break the illusions that bind you, and leave them behind you, as you see what is surely ahead of you. This is casting a spell by knowing that all is well.

SPELL BOUND

You are bound for glory, infinite beings, when you cast a wondrous spell. You have just summoned the power of All That Is to bring about the manifestation of your desires. A SPELL is simple: **S**imply **P**lace the **E**nergy of **L**ove in **L**ight. You broadcast a future event as you imagine it into being. Albert Einstein realized this when he said that imagination is more important than knowledge. The knowledge of what is or has been can shift. The past has nothing to do with your future unless you continue to create more of it in the now. NOW is all there is! Be consciously present in each new moment. *Be the cause of that which you want, because what you want is a reflection of who you are.*

See yourself as a gourmet chef concocting magical potions. If the recipe doesn't please you, do you curse the recipe? Or, do you play with it until you get it just right? You add different ingredients until the potion is just right. If you are steeped in the stew of the current view,

create something new! If you are notic-
ing that something is not in view, turn
now to thoughts that bring it to you.

Spells are binding contracts of creation,
unless you break the contract by offering thoughts of a contrary nature. And
if you stray from the spell, and see that
all is not well, simply recast the spell. It
not only spells relief from resistance, it
spells out what lies before you.

YOUR MAGIC WAND

Reawaken to the remembrance of *who you are*, for you are Wondrous Wizards and Master Magicians, complete with invisible magic wands. Your wand vibrates with the feelings behind your thoughts and words, and it has great MAGNETIC power. The tip of your wand projects a beam of light that magnifies the level of attraction wherever you point it. The more you wave your wand at something, the brighter this light beam glows. Using this process consciously, increases your power as a Wizard. Your magnetic wand is very powerful, Creators! Pay attention to where you are pointing it!

Pay attention to what you attend to, for that is your point of coming attraction. You may be pointing your wand at the exact opposite of what you want or desire. That can make you irritated, frustrated, mad and sad...and it does! You have done this so much that it feels normal. *If something does not serve you, do not serve it to yourself.*

Here is the Master Magician's greatest secret: it is the alchemy of the mind that transmutes all things to gold. If an aspect of your physical experience is less than golden, wave your wand towards what glimmers, and shine your light on that. Magicians bring the invisible desire to the visible dimension and cause that which is undesirable to vanish. Remember your full potential for infinite power. As Master Magicians, you continually turn nonphysical energy into physical form.

***CHOOSE ONLY WHAT
YOU DESIRE,
AND WATCH MAGIC
TRANSPIRE.***

THE WHOLLY GRAIL

As you emerged into the physical realm, you embarked upon your **G**lorious **R**eign **A**s **I**nfinite **L**overs. Recognize that you are here to live your Royal Reign on Earth as it is in Heaven. Revel in this opportunity to fill yourself to overflowing with everything that makes your heart sing, those things that you

most want, that represent who you are.
Rather than drink one drop of what you
don't want, fill yourself full of scrump-
tiously satisfying, delightfully delicious
feel good thoughts. When you feel good,
you are being the most authentic version
of you. Fall in absolute love with your
life, and dive into *the sea of all possibilities*. What you think is most possible
is probable. There you will find yourself
playing in the Wizard's Wonderland, and
you shall experience life on physical
Earth as it is in nonphysical Heaven.

Most seek fulfillment from something
or someone outside of self. Yet lasting
fulfillment can only come from within.
As you say: "If only things would

change...or "I need you to be a certain way so that I can feel better," you are looking outside of yourself for fulfillment, and that is a reversal of the creative process. Friends, hear this! You must first create the feeling of being happy. In this way you attract the energy to support the happiness you are creating. Set forth to change the chain of events, instead of remaining chained to events that change to more of the same. See the reflection of what you are becoming. *What you feel is REAL, and it is REALized as REALity.*

When you are thirsty for fulfillment, drink of that which you desire, and you have set energy in motion to fulfill that desire. Why continue to drink of things that do not quench your thirst? You only do this out of habit. Once you become aware of this, it is no longer a habit but a choice. Therein lies your power. As you drink of who you wholly, truly are, you drink in fulfillment. Offer yourself loving nourishment. Drink freely from the Wholly Grail within your heart, for it renews and revitalizes the Self, bringing you back to your natural state of pure love and happiness. When you fill yourself full of what you love, it allows the SOURCE of all those things to flow freely to you. As you drink of what you dream and desire, you go beyond what is and has been. Now the universe yields manifestations beyond your wildest dreams and imaginations.

When you have had your fill of unfulfillment, you will find the satisfying nourishment that comes from within. Sip from the soothing thirst-quenching grail. Be a glutton for good feelings. Fill yourself full of the stuff that you love. Then you will find that you cannot take in one morsel or drink one drop of anything less than who you are!

THE MAIN MESSAGE

You hold the key to ultimate bliss. My message is clear, so hear me here: *your feelings are the vibration that brings forth your creation.* In every moment in this physical reality, you are sending a message that is defining your reality as an extension of you. You are constantly sounding a note, broadcasting a vibration. Always, you are humming the tune of either 'having' or 'not having' what you desire. When you first focus your desire on something that you do not have, you will resonate with the perspective of not having it. You can create an energy shift to bring that which you desire into your experience by waving the wand of your limitless imagination. When you imagine that you are already experiencing what you desire, you are experiencing fulfillment. You are drinking from the Wholly Grail. To master this magic, practice continuously!

It is best to refrain from seeing the absence of things you desire or the presence of things that are undesirable.

You present yourself with a gift when you can sense the presence of a desire fulfilled. See yourself receiving what you want by imagining that it is already there. Pretending is not a popular pastime, but here I see a new trend. As you tend to pretending, you become as children entering the kingdom of heaven.

When you master the craft of fulfilling your dreams first from within, those dreams MUST become physical reality. Love yourself fully, regardless of outer conditions or circumstances, and you will come to know the Source of your soul's magic.…See yourself as the Wonderful Wizard you truly are. Be the unconditional lover that you came forth to BE.

LET THE MAGIC BEGIN~
IT ALL STARTS WITHIN.

MASTERING MAGIC

Radiating the resonance of unconditional love is the intention of all those who have attracted this message. You have come forth to teach one another to stay with the love, no matter what the conditions hold. *You are love* expressing and experiencing itself. This unconditional love stuff is the stuff of which you are made. It is the core of your very being. It is the highest, fastest frequency of vibration that you can exude while being physically incarnate.

When you resonate anywhere away from that core being, you will know it by the way that you feel. Unconditional love matches the vibration of your Inner Being, Higher Self or Oversoul. You more fully sense your Inner Being as you tap into the frequency that feels good. When you feel good you are glorifying God/Goddess, All-That-Is! You recognize your connection to the eternal Source of all things wonderful, therefore you feel wonder-filled. It is really that simple. A lover is what you came here to be. And when you are not being a lover to self first, by staying connected and feeling good, you are not being who you know yourself to be.

HOLD TO THE CONDITIONS YOU DESIRE, NO MATTER WHAT THE CONDITIONS HOLD.

As you start to play with this state of being an unconditional lover, you may find that it is simply not that simple...unless, of course, you make it easy, by being conscious of radiating this frequency of vibration at all times. This is what masters do.

Now it is time to recognize that the master dwells within your soul. Be that calm master within who is infinitely poised, centered, still and silent. Shed light on negative emotions. Know that those places that hold fear instantly respond to the flow of love.

When conditions present themselves as less than ideal in your view, what do you do? One way is to try to get by, by not reaching too high. You can attempt to harmonize with the reality you see. Why limit yourself to this version of what could be? For there is another way, a lighter way to play. *Masters love to face what is in their face, because they know what is in their face is in their vibration.*

And this is a key to transformation. Undesirable conditions don't control your experience. They are outside of you, and all your control comes from within. When you look at what you don't want, you draw those things to you. Connection is creation. So, connect to what you *do* want!

Unconditional love has nothing to do with putting up with conditions that are not the way you want them to be. That is conditional love. You must resonate with conditions the way you *want* them to be. As you do this, realities that do not represent you will fade away. Masters beam the dream as a broadcasting signal, no matter what conditions appear to be real. They know that if they hold their light on desirable conditions, they access their infinite power to manifest preferred realities.

Most of you want conditions to change so that you can feel good. That is magic in reverse. Cast this spell and you will do well: Find a way to feel good so the conditions can change. As you follow your heart and change the inner view, the outer will follow through.

If conditions are not acceptable, what would be acceptable? What kind of conditions would you love to see, personally or for humanity? Exercise your power as creator! As you exercise anything, it gets stronger. Imagine what a better life looks like. It is the most joy-filled step you can take towards the growth and evolution of your soul.

No matter how you have been conditioned, you can move mountains of unconditional love forward by tapping into the constant flow of love, under any and all conditions. There you will always find your Source. When you keep returning to the love, no matter what, you become saturated in that love. Life becomes increasingly easy and effortless.

As you stay with being and beaming the lover that you are, by imagining things that are the highest representation of you and others, you are radiating the resonance of unconditional love.

Masters know that the way they feel determines the strength of their connection to their natural state of well-being. They have integrated the life-giving principle within: conceive ideas, nurture their growth and give birth to same. They lovingly allow all things to be in their own time and place, starting with themselves. Masters know that true freedom comes from the release of resistance. They allow the manifestation of something to be their guiding light, to show them how they were thinking and feeling. They enjoy the process of creation and do not condemn their creations, because they see the correlation between their energy output and their experiential outcome. They take responsibility for their creations, knowing there can be no blame. They honor the secret wisdom they hold, by casting spells rather than pearls of wisdom before there time. They know that no One needs saving. They allow others their experiences. They teach through example. And in their wisdom, they know that in this Youniverse, there are no victims, only awesome creators.

ATTENTION SEED-SOWERS!

Know that every image you hold in your mind will be made manifest through you, for you cannot separate who you are from your Source energy. What you say is so, for these are the seeds you sow, and you shall reap the harvest thereof.

Birth to Earth, after seed, takes nine months. Once planted, you can't see the seed, yet it is taking form. Know that seeds of images and ideas must grow. Allow them to mature in the medium of time, and have a good time while they do so. Allow yourself to bask in the knowing that it is growing. With that kind of seed-sowing, you will reap a plentiful harvest. It is spiritualization of matter.

Believe me, you do not want instant manifestation when you launch your creation. You came here to fine-tune your creative ability, and in the process, experience tranquility. If every thought you had was equal to itself in experience instantly, you would be overwhelmed with contrary creating.

As you project thought that has never been, you are expanding and evolving All That Is, eternally. What an undertaking! You are the courageous ones who came forth to materialize spirit into denser forms. And, since this process is unfolding throughout eternity, why not surrender to the feel-good flow? It is the way that will take you to where you want to go!

Others cannot create for you or make you feel anything. Others can influence you, but you are ultimately in creative control. *Since your thoughts determine your experience, be deliberate in choosing them.* Look at the word "liberate" within deliberate. You are liberated to experience your full potential when you deliberately think thoughts. Therein lies your power, for you determine how you are feeling by what you are thinking.

If you think it is hard, you are validated in that thought! If you think it is easy to feel good, the Youniverse demonstrates that to you. Simply...

> *PAY ATTENTION TO*
> *WHAT YOU ARE*
> *PAYING ATTENTION TO,*
> *BECAUSE THE UNIVERSE*
> *IS ALWAYS PAYING*
> *ATTENTION TO YOU!*

FLOW-ER POWER

Now you are reawakening to and re-membering the power you possess. Know that in your unfolding, you are never alone, even if you choose to go it alone. You are always connected, even when you feel disconnected.

In the sixties and seventies, flower-power reigned; into the next millennium, it is flow-er power or the power of the endless flow of love. What is flowing from you is what matters, because your thoughts and feeling become matter.

FEELING GOOD IS ALL THAT MATTERS, BECAUSE ALL MATTER IS MADE FROM WHAT YOU FEEL.

It matters how you impact others, not so much how others impact you. You are the designer of your destiny in every moment. You are the center of the YOUniverse. *Pay attention to how you are flowing energy, rather than how it is being flowed to you.* If you choose to concern yourself or be bothered by conditions around you, you are surrounding yourself with more of the same. And remember, that which is like unto itself is drawn. What you love or fear, you draw to you!

All that vibrates in harmony with your core self manifests in your life sooner or later. Why not make it sooner? Begin now by simply thinking thoughts that feel good. The more you feel good, the more reasons you have to feel good.

Dare to adventure into whatever thrills and excites you. Dance with your destinies as you define what they are. Consider your wants, then name them to claim them. After you identify your desires, get your energy flowing in the same direction. All physical manifestation is evidence of how you have been flowing your FEELINGS.

You return to the Source of your limitless power when you see only that which you want to see in your experience. Turn your cheek so to speak. Seek only that which you want to find. Through your focus of attention, be it on a thing real or imagined, comes the process of creation. Everything responds to your thought processes.

Listen to your body. It can tell you what you have been thinking. When you tap into thoughts of appreciation, and stay with the love, you are in the feel-good flow. For, the truth of it is, you love to be loved and give love.

IF YOU ARE FEELING BLUE, YOU ARE NOT BEING TRUE BLUE TO YOU.

When you feel bad or blue, this is not you. If you are enthused and energetic, you are right on course. That is your inner guidance saying, "Yes!" Listen within, for when you are being/beaming who you are, life is bliss. Take this journey to the heart, to experience the feeling of having it all and not wanting for anything.

As a deliberate creator, differentiate between expectancy and expectation! To have an expectation is limiting. To be in a state of expectancy is unlimited. Your freedom lies in the exhilaration found in letting go, not of *what* you want, but of how, when, who or where will it come from. The details can trip you up, as you worry rather than wonder, fear what might come rather than love what is sure to come, and doubt rather than trust.

Remember that the dichotomy of Divine order is to order it without expecting it to be delivered in a certain way. Set forth your intention with great clarity; then release it to the Youniverse, and be ever ready to receive. There is great power in giving up the struggle and surrendering to your good. If you find yourself continually asking for the same things, you are not believing that they are already yours. Do not doubt yourself as a creator. Instead, trust that the Youniverse delivers in a way that surpasses your highest dreams. Trust it and let it go, then KNOW it to be so. And so it is!

SEXTIMONY

When you ponder what you wish to create, remember ecstasy is your natural state. Although it is not often viewed as such—outside of the sexual arena, that is. You can create with ease, for the wondrous joy of creation, when you are fully contained within the experience. After you arrive at your destination, the culmination or climax, you are then on to the next thing. Life is contained within the process of creating. Enjoy the journey, for the attainment of the goal is short-lived.

The union of nonphysical and physical is pure orgasmic bliss. As sexual beings, you allow yourselves the fullness of explosive ecstasy that is your birthright. Through sexuality you contact a place that is found in inner space. This is where you want to go to allow the consciousness of Spirit to flow. This brings great joy, for in these moments, you are feeling your unlimited power.

When you are in the act of making love, you are feeling your connection with All

That Is. During sexual expression, you become focused on feeling good. You embrace the present moment, fully enjoying the journey. Now consider this: you heighten your connection to your Divine Source in every situation, when you apply the ease of sexuality to any creation.

REALITY REBELS

When you rebel or push against the reality of what is already made manifest, you can do nothing but be that reality. If you find yourself saying, "I don't want that," know that as you try to push it away, it prevails. *Whatever you are not wanting is not going to go away, if you keep going that way energetically*. There is no power in resisting anything. The experiences in your reality reflect that. You are powerful beyond your current knowing. You will come to know that it is best to *FEEL* your way through life, imagining Royal splendor rather than pushing against things or against one another over ideas, beliefs and things. There is more than enough of everything for everyone. Rediscover the Source of all things wonderful, and bridge that from nonphysical (Spirit) into physical (Spirit densely defined). Nothing can become physical before it is seen (imaged) nonphysically. That is how you came into being, and that is the method of all creation. You are continually calling other creations into being in the same way. You are the creator of all that is real.

WHAT YOU FEEL IS WHAT IS REAL, AND WHAT IS REAL IS WHAT YOU FEEL.

You would be surprised how often you bring yourself to the brink with the thoughts that you think. Most of you are glued to your current view. Rarely do you look inside of you. Most of the time, you are so fixed on observing living reality that you get bogged down with practicality. If you buy into the illusion of what appears to be real, you've simply forgotten to flow what you feel. Create the inner-view anew, and break the illusions that blind you. You'll find the way to leave them behind, as you consciously employ your mind. Ask yourself this simple question:

WHERE AM I GOING ... WITH WHAT I AM FLOWING?

You can only get what you WANT as experience by turning your attention from what you *don't* want. Simply shift the energy. If you fear realities that may come to pass, what would you love to see at last? If you are nervous or scared, see that as excitement!

Look beyond what is; look to what is to be. A reality check is best left unchecked if it is not to your liking: it is irrelevant evidence. When undesirable conditions and circumstances become reality, use the power of your imagination to mold new realities. Imagine wellness where there is illness. Imagine prosperity where there is poverty. Imagine love where there is loneliness. Where there is suffering and sadness, see joy and jubilation. In doing this, friends, you make that potentiality into an inevitability.

When you start to play with deliberately directing energy, don't beat yourself up for having negative emotions. Love them, for they serve as your best friend

and spirit guide. Pushing against bad
feelings doesn't feel good. It will take
some time to turn your energy around.
Go easy on yourself with this new process of deliberate creation. You were
taught that it is normal to feel negative
emotions. Now you are remembering
how natural it is for you to feel positive
emotions.

MERLIN'S MATHMAGIC

Living life in Wizard's Wonderland is a matter of mathematics, a simple addition or subtraction, if you will. When you are focused on adding to your life, you feel inspired, uplifted, EXPANDED. You are acknowledging your unlimited nature. But when you start to subtract, you begin to contract. Now let us say that you want to add something, only because you want to subtract something else. Where is the dominant vibration headed, in the direction of what you. DO or DON'T want to add? *You only attract more of what you want to subtract.*

You cannot take away or subtract bad habits, you simply add what feels good, because that is who you are. Some may say that it feels good to attack or take revenge. Where are they taking themselves by the addition of such? They attract the attack. No one can defy or deny the law of attraction, what goes out must come back.

Life is always about experiencing more, not less. Anytime you take-away or subtract, you get less. Anytime you add, you get more. So, what is in store for you, mathematically speaking, more or less?....Keep adding, of course! *Keep in mind that you get to keep what you keep in mind*. When you focus on what you want to subtract, remember:

WHAT YOU ADD TO YOUR THOUGHTS, MULTIPLIES AND GROWS.

Add to the equation what you do want, along with more love, appreciation and praise for yourself. Master the craft of this math, for this formula equals ecstasy.

TIME-TRAVELING

Become fascinated with your future, as you live in the now. You are capable of accessing the future through the portal of your imagination. Time-travel can help you resonate with your ability to experience all that you desire.

As you reflect upon something from your past, *feel* that memory come alive.

You are breathing life into that memory *now*. All reality, past, present and future, occurs simultaneously in this moment. There is no other place that it can exist. You can travel into the past as you live it now. Those emotions are easily accessible.

Allow the power of your emotions to bring forth what you are wanting. You move energy in the direction of the scenarios you envision. With some practice, the ease of tapping into the past can be applied towards creating your future. You literally travel to another time as you live that future now! Imprint the future you desire as a memory, and it is done! Memorizing the future makes for magic, magicians!

Travel to the inner dimensions. Take a mind trip. Decide on a specific reality you would like to attract into your life. Simply design the dreamscape in which you see yourself living. Where are you? What are you doing? Who are you with? Take a mental picture of what that looks like—a *photo-thought*. As you project that future event, become emotionally involved in the scenario by *feeling it now*. Revel in the luxury of knowing this is you, by being there in your heart and mind, *now*. As you do that, you are deliberately placing yourself at the very center of creation. Getting all your physical senses fully involved encodes a powerful message in your cellular memory. It gets easier and easier to access, as it becomes a memory of what has been. Be detail-oriented about this…to the extent that it *feels good* to do so. What are the smells, tastes and sounds that make up your dream? Visit that reality again and again, just as if you were simply strolling down memory lane. Continue to refine these images over and over. Allow these visions to become like a vivid memory that you can easily recall at will. As you put your energy behind your future, you will see it manifest before you. Now you are mastering the magic of creation!

WHEN I WANT IT, I GET IT, BECAUSE I ALREADY HAVE IT!

To manifest, first *visualize*, then *familiarize* and *memorize*. Those things that you want are no longer outside of you. There is absolutely nothing separating you from your desires, energetically. As you say it exists, Creators, it exists! When the frequency of vibration emitted matches fulfillment, it can be no other way.

ROYAL REUNION

You are never separate, for all living things share the same life force. You are ONE. Have more FUN! Look around at all the diversity, then pick and choose what you'd like to experience. I only see you as who you are. If you choose to see yourself as anything less than wholly who you are, know that is your freedom to do so. When you make choices that take you further from your highest Truth, you will inevitably pick yourself up from those falls, and move again towards what you want to experience.

After falling, you will hear your Spirit calling. You rise to greater insight and clarity, because through that experience, you come to a fuller, more decisive knowing of what you DO WANT. Sometimes you have to experience what you don't want, to get what you DO want! This is wondrous, Wizards. *It has taken everything you have ever experienced to get you to where you are*. That was then, and this is NOW. All your power lies in the here and NOW. From out of the ashes of any unwanted event, comes the vision to see something more magnificent.

The one and only constant is *change*. The heart of evolution is: EXPAND AND INCLUDE. If you do that relative to everything, you then experience who you came here to be. You are consciousness expanding and including. You only contract to expand all the more.

> *There is only YES,*
> *the inclusion of all things at which*
> *you point your wand, wanted or not.*

What is it that you choose? As you give your attention to that which manifests in your experience, will it be magic or misery, pain or pleasure, agony or ecstasy, worry or wonder, sadness or happiness? Where will you place your focus?

FOCUS IS THE FIRE
THAT FUELS
THE COMBUSTION
OF CREATION.

CREATING CAMELOT

Enlightenment itself is a never-ending process. You are an artist extraordinaire. You ARE creative, for you cannot not be creative. There is no act in all the universe that is not creative. And a TRUE artist knows that the joy of creating is in the PROCESS, not in the result.

Life is not about where you are, what you have become or what happens to you. It is always about where you are going, what you are becoming and what you do with what happens to you. Use your powerful magic wand, potions, spells and time-travel to manifest your vision of who you want to be and what you want to do or have.

Call upon your free will to create peace in Camelot. Before you begin, find the calm center within. When you find yourself in need of anything, you are resonating in lack. Sickness exists only as the absence of wellness. Darkness is the absence of light. Poverty is the illusion of scarcity. In truth, there is no lack in all of Wizard's Wonderland. If you are looking at lack, that is what you get back. This serves you well, so you can better see what you have been up to within. As you play with this never-ending process, remember to keep it light.

You complain in vain, and it brings you more pain. "...my dad, my mom, my spouse, my kids, my job, my boss, my health, my car, my coffee, my finances, my fears, my failures, my nails, my neighbors, my difficulties, my struggles, my hair, my stress, my sacrifices, my concerns, my worries, my weight, my work...." My, oh my, how you do go on! As the Royal Rule of Reflection would have it, in your complaining you only bring more things to complain about. Keep in mind that all of life has both negative and positive aspects. *Your pointed wand is your point of view.* Friends, know that as you appreciate the aspects of life that feel good, you give more life to those realities. The better you feel, the better it gets!

When you feel bad, this is good. In that moment you are being alerted that you are resonating in harmony with the opposite of what you desire. Now, start your creative fire. Set your conscious sights on what you want. *You want things for the feelings they give, and you are only given those things when you know they are a given.*

I KNOW WHERE I AM GOING, BECAUSE I AM ALREADY THERE!

Where are you already there? In your imagination, where all deliberate creation first takes place.

For eons, you have been listening to each other rehash and reiterate old worn-out thoughts that no longer serve you. You, as a mass consciousness, have been creating "cycles of sameness" through hand-me-down habits and beliefs that are a disservice to mankind. You have largely forgotten your first and foremost nature: to be joyful. You have developed what you term "second nature." To a great extent, this is not your natural state of being but merely habits of thought. It seems completely normal to tell yourself and others how it is, what you experience, even if it isn't pleasant. You form groups to fight wars against all sorts of things. This is not how you intended life to be. It is how you were taught to be. Instead, speak of how you want it to be, how you would have it if you could have it your way. This is found within you, in the land of your dreams and visions. If you find you are feeling pain, consider then, what would be your pleasure?

There is vast untapped energy in the cocreative process. Remember that what you create together grows. Haven't you seen how focus on anything makes it bigger? Focus your increasing power on the good of all. Using your clearest intentions, rally together for realities that bring bliss.

As you release *fear, doubt* and *worry*, you get out of your own way, and allow the *YOU*niverse to go out of its way for you. The way of the wizard is *love, trust* and *wonder.*

More and more of you are beginning to use your power on purpose. Never, in the history of humankind, have there been more people at one time returning to their power. Get excited about the synchronicity of all your creations.

THE END OF ANYTHING
IS JUST THE BEGINNING

The power of creation is born anew in each moment. In your quest, the only question you need pose is this: Does that thought I just had feel good? *If it feels good, it's worthy of your Royal attention.* It freely allows your energy to flow through you. It equates with ease. Anything less is not worthy of your Royal attention. It freezes your flow, for it has nowhere to go, other than to where you don't want to go. Your only work as physical beings is to play. Engage your True Self in the game of life. The game of life is played by your rules, as you reflect upon how you want things to play out.

See yourself expressing your unique gifts. And this essential point must be clear, for this is why you have come here. Life wants what you have to offer. Present your offering to the world that waits. Your magic is Divine, and you are One of a kind. There has never been a more opportune moment than this, to resonate to the tune of bliss. Thrill to what lies ahead. Connected to your

Source, you can create anything. When you believe it, you shall have it. You were taught that *seeing is believing*, and what I want you to know is that *believing is seeing* it first.

When you fully know that you create everything, you can create anything! Whether your intended manifestation is big or small, use the energy of creation that flows through all. You can just as easily create a palace as a parking place. It is easy to manifest the object of your desire when you haven't a lot of resistance. Resistance has varying degrees of dominance, depending on how long you have allowed it prominence. Simply move into a receptive mode. Wave your magic wand, and point it at the reality you choose.

The physical realm is a plentiful playground. YOU are the physical connection to matches made in heaven. Give your sole (soul) attention to the current of joy from the unseen dimension. *To resonate with joy, allow yourself to become one with your desire. When you envision what you cannot see, you move to a new vibration of having it all. See beyond the visible range, and you will never vibrate apart from your desires.*

Desires manifest faster and more smoothly when you consciously align with Source first, rather than just taking action or forcing yourself to do it alone. Remove your powerful sword from the stone with the ease of Royalty. Access your Royal nature by acknowledging that anything you want to accomplish is already yours. Take it for granted. Anticipate the becoming. Be true to who you are at your core, the unconditionally loving you, your highest vision of yourself in every moment. Your only purpose is to live on purpose, by fully being yourself.

You are beaming Source energy with every thought and every breath. You need only recognize your limitlessness. In the forthcoming Wizard's Wonderland, we will offer you more ways to play your way to happiness.

Inevitably, you shall return home to your absolute power, for that is *who you are.* Your Inner Being cannot be taken away, for you were birthed from Source. You are continually birthing creations with all that you think and feel. Be in a constant state of celebration, APPRECIATION and GRATITUDE, and you will manifest an abundant life. Just relax, release and allow the rich flow to freely flow through you, as you guide it right to where you want to go. Life is a creative adventure.

Let us play!

*In closing, my gift to you is **Merlin's** "**Charm of Making**," to assist you in the manifestation of greater and more purposeful deliberate creations.*

"The Charm of Making" is seeing!

POINT—PRETEND— PREPARE—PRESTO...

POINT your magic wand at what you desire. Where you point your wand is your focus of attention. This is your coming attraction, magnetized to you and *through* you, magically. This wand vibrates with the thoughts and feelings you project from within. Remember that what you are thinking and feeling is always what you are matching as experience. Ask yourself what it is that your TRUE heart desires. Feel the power in making a decision. As a master magician, when you cast your spell, do so knowing that ALL IS WELL!

PRETEND it is here...fully seen and felt. This is harmonizing with *who you are*, who you know yourself to be. This is where you sing the song of fulfillment and hum the tune of already having what you desire. Hold a vision that is clear, then wave your wand towards what you hold dear. As you do this, you energize that nonphysical vision (light form) in becoming physical manifestation (dense form).

PREPARE yourself, for the manifestation of your desire is coming. What you have become cannot be undone.

PRESTO. There you have it! The making of what you desired, what you knew and felt you already had, *is now yours*!

MERLIN'S TEN COMMANDMENTS

~ I Commend You...

~ for assigning your signature vibration to only that which you want in your experience.

~ for greeting, meeting and matching your desires in your imagination, where there is no lack or neediness.

~ for pointing your wand only in the direction of your desires.

~ for heeding the focus of your attention.

~ for going with the flow and trusting where you'll go.

~ for only selecting from the reflective pool of polarities that which feels good.

~ for making matches that represent heaven, within your own mind.

~ for minding your own business of what is manifesting before you.

~ for going beyond what is, through the portal of your vast imagination.

~ for being fully present in your here and now.

Now play without ceasing!

"Dreamrise"
by Paula Sirois

In each day, throughout all your moments between time, allow your dreams to well up from within your heart. Breathe in the tender light that rises to the surface of your being on every sacred wave of wonder. And with the edge of your awareness, capture each strengthening whisper that passes before your Knowing....Pierce the unseen, and saturate yourself with the absolute recognition of full manifestation....Freely swim within the wide and immutable trust that is forever deepening. Grow forward in this rich and fertile condition where dreams are continually nurtured.

*Never cease to dream...for your dreams
define the joyful essence of who you
are and who you are becoming. This is
the fulfillment of timelessness in every
moment, to purely resonate with the
dream....Listen to the soulful tune of
Spirit, and hear its melodious notes
playing within the rhythm of your
heart. Speak your heart's message in
full measure that you may give shape to
all that you came here to BE.*

Look for upcoming books in the works by Marelin the Magician:

The *Wizard's Wonderland*, a course in how to deliberately create magic!

And more to come...

The Wizard's Wonderland

Marelin the Magician

ORDER FORM

To order copies of Merlin's Message or
8x10 color digital prints of cover art...

Send Check or Money order with this order form to:

Marelin the Magician
P. O. Box 747 • Tujunga, CA 91043

Please make checks payable to : **Power Play Shop**
(Prints are matted and signed by the artist)

QTY.	DESCRIPTION	AMOUNT
	Merlin's Message book(s)	**$5.00 ea.**
	Merlin's Message 8x10	**$16.00 ea.**
	SHIPPING & HANDLING	
	Add $3.00 for the first book ☞	
	Add $4.00 for the first print ☞	
	Add $2.00 for each additional item ☞	
	Calif. residents add 8.25% Sales tax ☞	
	TOTAL	

Your name_____

Address _____

City _____ State _____ Zip _____

ORDER FORM

To order copies of Merlin's Message or 8x10 color digital prints of cover art...

Send Check or Money order with this order form to:

Marelin the Magician
P. O. Box 747 • Tujunga, CA 91043

Please make checks payable to : **Power Play Shop**
(Prints are matted and signed by the artist)

QTY.	DESCRIPTION	AMOUNT
	Merlin's Message book(s)	**$5.00 ea.**
	Merlin's Message 8x10	**$16.00 ea.**
	SHIPPING & HANDLING	
	Add $3.00 for the first book ☞	
	Add $4.00 for the first print ☞	
	Add $2.00 for each additional item ☞	
	Calif. residents add 8.25% Sales tax ☞	
	TOTAL	

Your name _____

Address _____

City _____ State _____ Zip _____